REM 9/52

ALFRED GREGORY'S EVEREST

EVEREST
40th ANNIVERSARY
1953 - 1993

ALFRED GREGORY'S
EVEREST

————

WITH A FOREWORD BY
JAN MORRIS

CONSTABLE · LONDON

First published in Great Britain 1993
by Constable and Company Ltd
3 The Lanchesters
162 Fulham Palace Road
London W6 9ER
Copyright © 1993 Alfred Gregory
ISBN 0 09 472240 4
Printed in Great Britain by
BAS Printers Ltd, Over Wallop, Hampshire

A CIP catalogue record for this book
is available from the British Library

FRONTISPIECE:
Patterns in the Icefall

TITLE PAGE VERSO:
Mount Everest, the South Col, the Lhotse Face and the
 Khumbu Icefall

CONTENTS PAGE:
Sunlight and clouds of Khumbu

DEDICATION PAGE:
The Western Cwm, once a secret corner of Everest

CONTENTS

To
MY WIFE SUZANNE

FOREWORD

This book records one participant's responses to a minor but unusually happy historical event – the first ascent of Mount Everest, the highest place on earth, in the summer of 1953. Nothing was greatly changed by this achievement: as the climber H. W. Tilman wrote of mountaineering achievements in general, quoting G. K. Chesterton, their attraction is that they are perfectly useless to everybody. The first ascent of Everest was a footnote, rather than a heading, and its charm lay in its innocence.

Sport could still be innocent then, and John Hunt's team of Britons, New Zealanders and Sherpas went to Everest that year almost boyishly. Of course, after 40 years of failures on the mountain, they badly wanted to succeed. Of course they hoped that a British expedition could pull off the first ascent, especially as 1953 was to be the Coronation year of Queen Elizabeth II, fondly hailed as the start of a new Elizabethan era. Of course the climbers wanted to be famous, and the porters needed their pay. But the expedition still went to Everest essentially for the fun of it, and it went as a proper team, without prima donnas or transfer fees, anxious only that some of its number, no matter who, got to the top. When Edmund Hillary and Tenzing Norgay did, Hunt declined to speak of the Conquest of Everest: terrifying though it could be, and estranged from mankind over so many millenia, the mountain was never an enemy.

Three people, throughout the expedition, assiduously recorded the scene. Two of us were professionals. Tom Stobart the film cameraman had made documentary movies around the world, and as the correspondent of the *Times*, the only reporter there, I was the archetype of your insufferably ambitious young foreign correspondent. The third

observer, though, was a pure amateur. It was not simply that Alfred Gregory, who was in charge of the still photography, was not really there as a photographer, but as one of the toughest and most experienced of the climbing team: it was also that, whether he was working out exposure rates or hacking steps in the ice at 28,000 feet, he brought to everthing the guileless enthusiasm of one who does things for the love of doing them.

One could hardly help enjoying going to Everest. The long trek through the exquisite lowlands, at that time almost unknown to outsiders – the friendliness of the Sherpas and the seduction of their Buddhist faith – the fascination of the long glacier approach, the mystery of the Tibetan heartlands beyond – the tumbled labyrinth of the icefall – the glory of the high snowfields – the brilliant blue skies and dazzling stars – the grand plume of driven snow which flared like a triumph from the summit – above all the presence of the great mountain itself, the top of the world, the culminating earthly objective – all these would have made the adventure a glory and an excitement for the most world-weary dullard.

Upon Alf Gregory they had, I think, a truly transcendental effect. He was already a man of unusually varied background. He had been climbing since his boyhood, in the Lake District, in the Alps, and in 1952 in the Himalaya itself. He had worked as a printer's apprentice, run a travel agency and been an officer in the Black Watch. Far from making him blasé, though, all this seems only to have sharpened his sensibilities. Nothing ever bored him. I remember him on Everest moving always with a sharp eagerness, always on the move, always looking at things, rather like a Lancashire terrier in the pink of condition. As he says in this book, the

nobility of the scenes around him, the
excitement of the moment, made him see
everything in a new way, and in his attitude
to the mountain itself he was perhaps closer
to the Sherpas, who considered its summit
divine, than to those of us who thought of it
merely as a mountaineering prize, a fine sight
or the possible subject of a scoop.

Most of Gregory's photographs, his record
of these responses, have remained unseen for
forty years. Those that have previously been
published have all too often been unworthily
reproduced. It is only now, in this volume,
that we can see for ourselves how grandly
the experience of Everest touched him, how
exuberantly he brought his artist's eye to that
most tremendous of places, and how truly he
has captured for us the exploit of happiness,
the act of reconciliation perhaps, that was
Everest, 1953.

JAN MORRIS

INTRODUCTION

One recent Sunday morning, my friend Les Peel arrived at my home in the Peak District and handed me an article from the press asking, 'Have you seen that?' I read with astonishment how, in the spring of 1992, thirty-two people had reached the summit of Mount Everest on one day; climbers had actually queued to negotiate the famous Hillary Step on the final ridge to the top; and down at Base Camp there was chaos with thirteen different expeditions all attempting the same South Col route. Is this what we climbed Everest for? Perhaps it is. More and more people will want to go to the top of the highest mountain in the world and there is no way this can be changed, but how much can Everest take without the whole of this pristine wilderness being completely destroyed?

Back in the early 1950s we knew we had the whole of the Himalaya to ourselves; we were marking the high snows with our footprints where no one had been since the earth was made, and Everest was still the loneliest place on earth. As we climbed into the secret corners of this mountain we did not give a thought to what might happen to it afterwards. Of course the first ascent of Everest in 1953 had a great impact on the mountaineering world and it became the springboard from which climbing as a sport then took off. As the years went by more and more people went out on the hills and mountains, until today they are numbered in hundreds of thousands. So it is not surprising that we now find crowds in what was once lonely country. Perhaps it is not surprising to find queues on Everest! Maybe we are to blame – but no doubt it would have happened anyway.

(Left) Porters in the foothills.

I was invited to join the 1953 Everest team as a climbing member of the party and then later, because of my interest in photography, I was asked to take charge of stills photography. On the long walk from the Kathmandu Valley to the mountain I worked closely with Tom Stobart (who made the Everest film) for we had so much in common. Together we wandered slowly through wonderful foothill country, looking in a leisurely manner for pictures to illustrate our story and sharing thoughts about exposures and the correct lighting for our film.

Most members of the team had cameras and took pictures on the mountain; this meant we could obtain full coverage of the expedition. My particular job was to make sure we got that cover whilst shooting as much as possible myself. Of course I could not photograph everything that happened, I could only record the events taking place around me, and at the same time I tried to do justice to the incredible splendour of the landscape and the beauty of a virgin mountain wilderness swept by the wind and scorched by the sun.

I have always wanted to present my black and white pictures from this great expedition in my own way but the negatives have not been available to me. Owing to the arrangements under which the Everest black and white pictures were held I have had no access to them and it was only in the autumn of 1991 that I saw them for the first time since 1953. It was certainly one of the most exciting and satisfying moments in all my years of photography when I had my beloved negatives in my own professional darkroom and I could print my pictures the way I had visualized when I shot the film so many years before. Many of my pictures were used over and over again in books and periodicals immediately after the expedition, but in forty years no one has printed them with the same care as I would give to them myself, nor made big archival exhibition prints (apart from a limited number made by Kodak in the 1950s). I cannot describe the thrill and excitement this gave me. For some weeks I worked almost day and night making enlargements. Only those who are used to working with black and white will understand the wonder of seeing a print slowly forming in the developer, and then, like a piece of magic, a superb image appears on the paper. I found I had been right to shoot on fine-grain film like Panatomic X for the pictures taken with my Rolleiflex are grainless. It is also satisfying to be able to print on the superb quality fibre-based paper which is produced today.

As a professional photographer I was distressed at the condition of many of the negatives; they were very badly scratched, but with long hours of careful retouching I have tried to rectify this. And so I have been able to put together a personal collection of photographs from one of the greatest periods of my life. Most of the pictures have never been published before and to enhance my story I have included just a few taken when I was on other expeditions during the 1950s to the Himalayan kingdom of Nepal.

In order to illustrate my own personal 'Everest' I have included photographs which meant a great deal to me at the time when I shot them; my memories are still vivid of the huge effort required to take a picture at 27,000 feet. I can clearly recall the glory of a pristine wilderness across which black shapes struggled under great loads, and, in contrast, I remember the relaxed and carefree days of walking through forested foothills where we had breathtaking glimpses of distant ice peaks.

Two pictures in particular made a great impression on me and brought memories flooding back: the breathtaking beauty surrounding a huge crevasse behind Camp 3 where Wilf Noyce is crawling across a ladder which bridged it, and the immense wilderness of the Western Cwm where the black shapes of Wilf and Sherpas were starkly etched on a two-dimensional white world as they moved along the side of another crevasse of bottomless depths. These were taken during the period when I spent a very happy time with Wilf and the Sherpa porters ferrying stores from Camp 3 at the top of the Icefall to the head of the Western Cwm to establish Advance Base Camp. For about a week we were on our own in that great lonely wilderness which was the remote inner sanctuary of Everest; its awesome beauty made a lasting impression upon me.

The last time I had seen my films was when I packed them up and handed them to a runner somewhere high in the Himalaya in 1953. And so, after almost forty years, my dreams of my book have become a reality.

Fate had put me on Everest with a camera and it was up to me to make the most of this opportunity. Was I just going to take simple record pictures or could I develop some form of personal artistic expression in this high white wilderness? Of course I had to cover as fully as possible the details of the expedition, the mountains themselves and the actions of our actual climb. But Everest was a completely new experience – it was photography on an awesome scale. I realized I was shooting the story of a great adventure although I certainly did not have the foresight to know I was shooting history. And there was so much more besides. I had the power to make images which, apart from illustrating James Morris's articles for the *Times*, could tell more than just a tale of action on the mountain. Through imagery seen with the lens I could attempt to convey what climbing on Everest was all about in spite of the altitude, the weariness and lassitude which come to all when high on the mountain. I had the opportunity to say

Prayer flags and a chorten near the Sherpa village of Khumjung.

something special, not just factual statements, but something intimate and personal about this tremendous mountain and the wonderful scene continually in front of me.

To do all this meant working when I was dog tired from a day's hard climbing, forcing myself out of my tent when all I wanted was to lie back in a sleeping bag and rest. It meant worrying about keeping cameras warm and so I had to sleep with them; they are uncomfortable bedfellows. As on all photo assignments, it was easy to think of the pictures which got away and I worried continually whether there were enough good photos to tell the whole story and be a true pictorial account of what was to become an historic event.

Back in the 1950s nearly all press photography was on large format cameras; the widespread use of 35mm film was still in its infancy. Today it seems strange to recall that the *Times*, which had world rights on the publication of our expedition story, could not then handle film smaller than 5 × 4 in their darkroom and that all their staff photographers worked in that format. It was therefore necessary to re-equip their darkroom to process the 35mm and 120-roll film which I had chosen to take to Everest. I knew it would be impossible for me to carry a large, heavy 5 × 4 camera on the climb as well as the big tripod which would have been necessary with that size camera. My decision delighted the head of the *Times* darkroom as he now had an excuse to modernize his equipment, and he rang to thank me for making this possible. But doubts lingered. The picture editor was very worried about 35mm film and sent me a Super Ikonta camera ($2\frac{1}{4} \times 3\frac{1}{4}$) which he said he would prefer me to use! It was a good camera with a beautiful Zeiss lens but with its bellows it was awkward and I found it clumsy to use in the difficult cold conditions high on Everest.

My 35mm cameras were a Contax and a Kodak Retina 2. The Contax, with 50mm and 125mm interchangeable lenses, was my main camera for colour but when I went high on the South-East Ridge, to almost 28,000 feet, I carried the more compact Retina up to the highest camp. Throughout that day I only shot Kodachrome from which excellent black and white negatives were made later.

I also took a twin-lens Rolleiflex which I used for black and white. Despite being more bulky than the Contax and Retina it was extremely easy to use and with its superb Zeiss lens it was capable of producing pictures of exquisite quality; I took it as far as the South Col and the final results made the extra effort well worth while. When in recent years these three cameras were stolen I felt I had lost a very real part of history.

Cameras with automatic focus and exposure control did not exist in 1953 and so everything was performed manually. It was of extreme importance to determine the correct exposure and I carried a Western Master exposure meter which I used with an incident light attachment for much of the time. My greatest worry on Everest concerned these exposures. By the end of the expedition I felt I had done everything right but there was a tiny niggle of doubt; did I always react correctly under the pressures created by living for a long time at high altitude? Had I done anything silly? Tom Stobart was just as worried about his cine film. I had received a few reports from England which said the exposures were correct but the only films they had received were those shot in the valleys during our march in to the mountain. The climb was over and we were back at Base Camp before I knew anything about pictures taken above the snow line. It was here that we began to receive the first telegrams of congratulations and the one I liked best was worded: KODACHROME BATCH RECEIVED RESULTS EXCELLENT CONGRATULATIONS KODAK.

By 1953 colour film, and in particular Kodachrome, had begun to make an impact on the photographic scene, but newspapers and magazines relied on black and white. With the fast film available today it is interesting to recall the only Kodachrome film then on the market was rated Weston 8 (ASA 10!). Black and white film was a little faster; in my Rolleiflex I shot with Kodak Panatomic X, rated at Weston 25 (ASA 32). Films were rated Weston because of the widespread use of the Weston exposure meter.

I recall what is now an amusing anecdote which concerned 35mm colour film. When we were back in Britain all members of the team were called upon to give many lectures and I shall never forget the first one given by John Hunt, Ed Hillary and myself in the Festival Hall, London. I was given the job of making the projection arrangements. Because it was believed to be impossible to project 35mm slides across such a big hall, Kodak specially made $3\frac{1}{2} \times 3\frac{1}{2}$ inch slides from the chosen 35mm transparencies. These were of beautiful quality but when I tried them out in the Festival Hall the light output from the projector was so dismal that I hastily telephoned Kodak, who then offered another projector (a Kodak Master): the lecture was a tremendous success using the original 35mm Kodachromes. This was another first, because slides of this size had never before been used for such a big show in Britain.

To tell my tale of Everest I should perhaps mention that my first summit was Pendle Hill in Lancashire! I was very young when I went up the sharp end from the village of Downham. When I started to work I saved and bought a bicycle which gave me the freedom to go wherever I wished. One day I caught up with another cyclist on the long journey home and noticed he had boots strapped to the back of his bike. I began to chat with him and he told me he had been fell walking in the Lakes. That seemed to me to be a very exciting idea and so I bought some boots; my love affair with the hills had begun. I soon realized that unless I started rock climbing I would be denied access to some of the most exciting terrain in the district. In those days there were very few people climbing and I knew most of the climbers I met on the crags. This was in the '30s, long before I had started to dream of the Himalaya. I had very little money but that did not matter for I had everything I needed for a life of adventure – good health, physical fitness, a bicycle, a pair of climbing boots and a rope.

In those early years before the last war the only way I could go rock climbing was to cycle to the Lake District, but that was my greatest joy as I was a dedicated cyclist before

I was a climber. At the time I was working in the printing trade where, because of a strong union, we were the first people to win a five-day week. This, combined with the start of the Youth Hostel Association, opened for me a new world. Leaving work at 6 p.m. on a Friday evening, I could spend the weekend where I wished – but especially I could get on my bike and pedal alone the 75 miles from my home in Blackpool to the Lake District and the glory of the hills.

In my memory it was very often pouring with rain and it was a long hard ride to Langdale and the barn at Side House Farm. On arrival I would walk into the house: the door was always open, for the family did not possess a key. As I went into the kitchen the farmer, Bob Birkett, would appear at the top of the stairs wearing a long night-shirt and shout down, 'Is that thee, Alf? Reet, then brew thi sen a cup of tea.'

In his barn it was dry and warm in the hay and I always slept well. True, a rat ran over me now and then but it did not matter. Saturday was a day for long hard training walks alone on the Lakeland tops, possibly doing all the 3,000-footers before returning to Langdale. That evening I would be joined by my climbing companions who had cycled up after work; they were not so lucky as I, for they worked on Saturday mornings.

On Sunday we were up in the dark and after cooking a quick breakfast we were away very early to make the most of the day before cycling back to Blackpool. We climbed hard in those days and filled every minute with dedicated effort. In winter it would almost certainly be dark before we came off the hills. Over at Coniston on Dow Crag, climbers arriving at the rocks at a more civilized hour used to call us 'the Dow Crag night shift'. It always seemed a long ride back, and I would reach home any time between 11 p.m. and 2 a.m. the next morning. Needless to say, I would be very tired indeed going to work on Monday.

In those days specialist climbing gear was

unknown; there were no waterproof coats nor windproof anoraks. We wore cord breeches and a second-hand tweed jacket with the lapels fastened up with a safety pin. Wool socks, hats and jerseys were knitted by my mum. We climbed in boots with tricuni or clinker nails in the soles – rubber vibram did not come until after the war. I wore Timpson's boots which cost £1.50 a pair, while my choice for nails was Ortler clinkers which I used to buy from Bob Laurie, the celebrated boot maker in Burnley. We carried rubber plimsolls tucked into our waistband for use on the harder routes but even the difficult climbs we tried to do in nails just to make them harder. Thus they became training climbs for when we went to the bigger peaks of the Alps, or, should our dreams come true, to the Himalaya. For us, rock climbing was not an end in itself but a form of training which would hopefully lead one day to big expeditions in the highest mountains of the earth.

All young men have heroes and in those days mine were all Himalayan men: Shipton, Smythe, Mallory, Norton, Sommerville, all great names who had been high on Everest. Little did I think the years would roll by, a war would come and go, Everest would still remain unclimbed and the day would arrive when I too would be asked to join an expedition to attempt to climb the world's highest mountain.

It was in late 1951 when I heard a rumour that something was afoot in the world of Himalayan climbing and an expedition was being mounted to climb Everest. In the spring of that year Eric Shipton had led a team of climbers to Nepal to make a reconnaissance of the south face of the mountain and they had returned showing there was indeed a possible route via the Khumbu Icefall. Nepal had only recently opened its borders to the outside world after remaining closed to visitors for more than a hundred years, and all the earlier expeditions to Everest had approached it from Tibet on the north side of the mountain.

It was during the summer of the same year that one of my best friends, Archie Wavell, a fellow officer in my former regiment The Black Watch, had been climbing with me in the Alps. He had bumped into Eric Shipton whom he had previously met in Delhi and in the course of conversation about Everest

Eric Shipton in 1952.

Archie told him he ought to be taking me with him. In those years the number of mountaineers with the necessary Himalayan experience was not great. Men who had climbed on Everest in the pre-war days (with the exception of Eric Shipton) had passed the age group for such an endeavour. Already, I had three seasons climbing the classic routes of the Alps before the war, and even before the war was finally over I was able to go back on Alpine peaks. Once I was out of the army I returned to the Alps and climbed there winter and summer. Archie persuaded me to pass on all these details to Eric.

Then, on 30 January 1952, I received a telegram: 'GREGORY TRAVEL BLACKPOOL' HIMALAYAN CTTEE INVITE YOU TO JOIN COMING EXPEDITION EXPENSES PAID SAILING MARCH 7 PLEASE REPLY SHIPTON OBTERRAZ LONDON.

Please reply! I could scarcely wait to send off my acceptance. Inviting people to join an expedition by telegram had always been traditional since the early days of Everest expeditions; it was also customary to reply in the same way.

This expedition was to Cho Oyu in Nepal Himalaya and it actually took me into the mountains of the Everest region. It was basically to test the ability of men in the team to climb at high altitudes and so form a nucleus of climbers for an Everest expedition the following year. During the earlier part of the journey this put me, and I think the others, under some stress to prove I could do it, but as the expedition wore on all this was forgotten in the sheer joy of climbing and exploring at altitudes higher than any I had ever attained before.

To reach Cho Oyu we did not even bother to go through Kathmandu and we walked into Nepal from Jaynagar on the Indian border directly south of our mountain. Today this seems strange: a party would now be obliged to enter via the capital to collect the necessary permit after paying a large sum of money to the Nepalese Government for this permission.

When I joined the team at Jaynagar I was thrilled to find we had Ang Tarkay as our Sirdar, a legendary figure from the early Everest expeditions. His first job was to send our suitcases to Nepal where we would find them after the expedition was over. To my amazement he collected a few local porters, put our cases on their backs and told them to take them to the British Embassy in Kathmandu, explaining that they would be paid when they arrived. As I never expected to see my luggage again it was with incredulity that I found all my clothes hanging in my room when I eventually reached the Embassy some sixteen weeks later. Other Sherpas meeting us in Jaynagar were later to become famous men of Everest and to share our climbing for many years to come. Some, like Annallu and Dawa Tenzing, became extremely close personal friends.

Before we set off it was felt the porters we were engaging were asking too much money as they wanted 4 rupees a day, much more than the going rate for a load of 30 kilos. However, when we discovered they expected to carry 40 kilos (their normal loads were actually even more than that), we hurriedly packed everything and left for the hills!

I experienced a wonderful sense of freedom as I walked for the first time through the Himalayan foothills. These were days when we could climb any mountain we saw and explore any unknown valley we found. This freedom to wander more or less at will lasted throughout 1955 when I led an expedition to Rolwaling Himal where we climbed nineteen peaks and made a plane table survey of the area, and into 1958 when I went to climb Ama Dablam.

The first time I ever went high was early in the expedition when Charles Evans and I crossed a pass at about 19,000 feet in order to look at the south side of Cho Oyu before descending to a previously unexplored glacier. I shall never forget the thrill of just being there at the highest altitude I had ever reached and experiencing the breathtaking view from the pass where we camped, for we were looking out across a vast expanse of remote mountain country with range after range of ice peaks never before seen which stretched as far as the eye could behold. Years later I was to know most of this country extremely well but then it was all new and the most fantastic mountain vista I had ever seen.

To reach our route on Cho Oyu we had to cross over the border into Tibet and the closeness of the Chinese worried us a lot. This greatly inhibited us in our attempt on the mountain which in fact we did not climb. However, instead, we had time to visit part of the vast area of unexplored country which lies to the west of Everest. With Eric Shipton and Charles Evans I crossed a new pass, the Langmoche La, which gave access to the virgin Tolam Bau Glacier. Here we were surrounded by incredibly beautiful unclimbed ice peaks and from a base on the glacier we made a number of first ascents.

For me, one of the greatest thrills of this journey was the view from the top of the Tolam Bau Glacier. All the giants of the Himalaya stretched out before us; straight ahead were the peaks west of the Nangpa La and beyond them Tibet. We could see Cho Oyu and the wild range to the east past Gyachung Kang; and unmistakeable, solid and mighty, there was Everest black against the Himalayan sky – my first view ever of the world's highest mountain. Its left edge was the North Ridge which swept up from the North Col past the yellow band to the top. The right-hand side fell away past the South Summit and down the South-East Ridge to the South Col, before the rest of the southern route was hidden by the dramatic wall of Lhotse and Nuptse. So many of the peaks I was to know well were there in front of me that morning, Pumori, Ama Dablam, Kang Taiga – the fairy castle mountains of Khumbu. It was an unforgettable sight.

The whole of this journey was a wonderful introduction to the high peaks of Himal. For

three months I had been able to explore a vast area of unknown country. I felt I had acclimatized well to high altitude and was ready to go back. What memories the Himalaya was to hold for me during the epic days of the following year, and little did I think then that I would be able to return to this glorious land at regular intervals throughout the next forty years.

Nepal, compared with the tourist destination it has become, was a very different place in those days. Its frontiers had only recently opened to the outside world; few people had been permitted to go there when we arrived in 1952 and Khumbu, the region of Mount Everest, was remote indeed. Even to reach the Kathmandu Valley meant walking for two days across the foothills from India and on our arrival in the valley after such a journey we truly felt we had come to a mysterious land.

The city of Kathmandu was certainly not much more than a big village. There was no road from the outside world and no airport. The only way goods could come into the valley was on the backs of porters or by the 'ropeway' which transported supplies over the hills from India. There were no cars in the streets – in fact we would say in later years that more people had carried part of a car into the valley than had ever ridden in one – and the steps leading up to the ancient Buddhist temples and Hindu shrines were always spread with fresh vegetables brought into the capital by country farmers. The idea of tourist stalls with their fantastic array of goods and artefacts to tempt the foreigner was still many years away. And as there were no hotels we stayed at the British Embassy as guests of the Ambassador.

It was the same too in the mountains of Khumbu. Apart from Houston and Tilman in

Taleju Temple, Kathmandu.

1950, the 1951 British Reconnaissance and the Swiss in 1952, no Western parties had been there; it was remote country peopled only by Sherpas. When in 1953 we walked across the foothills we felt the whole of the Himalaya was ours for we met only Nepalese tribal people who lived in the foothill regions. Wherever we went we attracted a great deal of attention. Children stopped to stare and men and women looked at us with amazement. I am sure we presented a curious sight as we walked through the country swinging our big black Nepalese umbrellas – useful against hot sun and sudden rain showers. We grew accustomed to local men walking very close behind us, watching absolutely everything we did. We played a game amongst ourselves by suddenly stopping on some pretext so they were forced to pass, but, as they had all the time in the world, they would merely pause until we moved on and there they were, one step behind again. When we reached Namche people came from far away to sit all day long and watch everything we did. Never did we have a rubbish problem because any item we did not want became a collector's piece: an empty tin was a prized container for a local family. However, there is no doubt that some of the gear we were obliged to leave behind on the mountain was the beginning of a true litter problem which has accumulated over the years because of the number of expeditions which go annually to Everest.

For some years afterwards when we trekked through other remote areas of Nepal there was the same astonishment and amazement when people who had never before seen a Westerner met us coming down the trail. Sometimes a man, an ex-Gurkha soldier, would stop ploughing his field and stand to attention, for the only foreigner he would expect to see in his country would be a visiting Gurkha officer. Even fifteen years later when my wife, Sue, and I trekked beyond Pokhara and Ghorepani we met no one other than the local villagers. We travelled with a Sherpa who cooked our food and generally looked after us, and took just one porter to carry our gear. At night we slept on the verandahs of local houses and received unreserved hospitality in the villages. How many thousands of trekkers travel today through this area which is the most visited in the whole of Nepal? Everywhere one finds innumerable tourist lodges and tea-shops; the local people now refrain from welcoming a stranger to their tiny homes because their hospitality has been abused by their light-fingered guests and their possessions have disappeared into some foreign rucksack. What changes have occurred as the years have passed!

The many visits I have made to Nepal since those Everest days have allowed me time to look at the country and learn a very great deal about its culture and religion. The Himalayan mountaineer may not always appreciate the land through which he passes and so he learns little of the ways of its people. The average climber can be very single-minded in his desire to reach the high mountains and for me, in those early days, it was the same. Only much later did I realize I had fallen in love with Nepal, not just with its high peaks but with the people and their whole way of life, their traditions and religions, and, of course, with the staggering beauty of the foothills and high mountains. I wanted to return continually to capture all this wonder with a camera. When I now go to Khumbu young Sherpas ask me, 'Is this your first visit?' There is always a look of disbelief on their faces when I tell them I have been coming for forty years and their fathers and grandfathers were my porters and companions on the early expeditions.

After our 1952 journey, the leader of the 1953 Everest expedition was Eric Shipton; under his leadership Charles Evans, Tom Bourdillon and I were to be the nucleus around which the team was to be built in the

UK, with Ed Hillary and George Lowe joining us from New Zealand. Back in the UK Charles Evans and I were asked by Eric Shipton to choose this new team as Eric had been away for a long time in south-west China and he felt we knew the potential climbers better than he did.

Later, at Eric's request, I took a group to the Alps as a preparation for the selection of the Everest team. It really did not achieve much because bad weather interfered with our plans, but we all had a lot of fun and a superb holiday. Eventually the leadership of the Everest team was taken over by John Hunt, and then Charles and I had to wait to be invited to the team by John himself.

The story of the first ascent of Everest has been told many times, and wonderfully so by John Hunt in *The Ascent of Everest*, so this book is no place to go over again the tale of that historic climb. All I can do is to try to convey some of my personal memories while on the mountain.

As we moved up through the labyrinth of ice pinnacles in the notorious Khumbu Icefall and past deep crevasses and the incredibly steep walls of the Western Cwm, none of us had any idea who might make the summit attempt. When I gave thought to it, which was often, I made a resolve to try to go as high as possible and hope to perhaps reach the magical height of 28,000 feet, somewhere near the altitude gained by my childhood heroes of the pre-war attempts, Mallory, Smythe, Norton and Sommerville. Meanwhile, as each new day dawned it was simply a matter of getting on with the jobs of climbing and photography.

The Khumbu Icefall is the most complicated and the most dangerous problem on the mountain with over 2,000 feet of steep ice where enormous blocks move and fall at any hour of the day or night, making it a very frightening place. It has cost more lives than any other section of mountain anywhere in the world. Everybody in our team has vivid memories of moving through this tortuous and fearsome glacier; to me it always seemed at its worst in the afternoons when I made my way down through falling snow, extremely tired from long hours of ferrying loads up it to a higher camp.

It really was an horrendous place and, like everyone else, I had some narrow escapes. On one occasion, when I was about half-way up it, I was with some Sherpa porters and we were moving along the edge of a big crevasse. Suddenly, an enormous block of ice, about the size of a house, detached itself and started sliding towards us, gaining speed every second. It all happened so quickly that there was no time to be scared, and indeed there was nothing I could do apart from hope it would miss us. It reached the top of the slope immediately above, where it toppled over and dropped into the crevasse directly in front of where we stood, no more than a few yards away. Towering over us it teetered forwards and then settled as it wedged itself firmly into the crevasse. We breathed again and recommenced our climb – routine stuff, I thought, and all in a day's work.

There was an entertaining incident when I was leading a group of porters up from Base Camp to Camp 3 at the top of the Icefall. We had just crossed a wide crevasse by means of a snow bridge. I don't remember exactly how many porters were with me but the last man was Changju, who had been with me the year before in 1952 and had already become an old friend; like most Sherpas, he had a great sense of humour. To my horror, all of a sudden I saw Changju untie from the rope and jump down into the crevasse where he landed on a large piece of ice which was precariously jammed across a terrifying and bottomless hole. There he stood, seemingly without a care, and he then reached up to help the other Sherpas across the narrow snow bridge above him. When they were all safely over he climbed out, tied himself back on the rope and joined us – the devil looks after his own.

For all its hazards the Icefall was a very

beautiful stretch of mountain scenery, a fascinating world of white abstract shapes, where deep in the inner recesses of the crevasses lay mysterious pools of blue light, sometimes pastel, sometimes dark. It was this blue which dominated every detail of form and shape I saw on Everest, especially so when I looked up to where ice peaks were sharply etched against the azure sky. Even when it snowed, which was most afternoons, and the mountain was lost in a white-out, this subtle colour was there, influencing my thoughts about the beauty of this place. All this sounds as if I were only shooting in colour but for black and white work the feeling and the effect were the same: in the special monochrome pictures which Everest produced, blue became black (even with the lightest of filters) and the contrast of dark against light made for powerful imagery.

At the beginning of May it was decided that we should have a few days' rest, and we descended to Lobuche at about 15,000 feet. For one or two members of the team who had been unwell this was a good idea, but for me it was less so; I felt that I lost acclimatization by going lower and indeed I suffered quite a bit when I eventually struggled back up to Base Camp. However, there was a most memorable event when we were at Lobuche: we had a radio and I remember listening to the last few moments of the Cup Final with Stanley Matthews running down the wing to pass the ball to Stan Mortenson in centre to score two spectacular goals in the last minutes of the game. It was my home town, Blackpool, winning the FA Cup! And in later years the two Stanleys and I became firm friends.

I was delighted to be back at Base Camp. I had a great feeling of confidence in my personal fitness and there was the added excitement of being asked by John Hunt to go up in support of the second summit attempt by Hillary and Tenzing. There was no doubt in my mind that I should be able to go very high on the mountain to do this: it was very

exciting indeed to know that I was going up there and would be closely associated with events near the summit.

On 23 May, Tom Bourdillon and Charles Evans left Advance Base Camp at the head of the Western Cwm for the South Col from where they were to make the first assault on the summit. Using closed-circuit oxygen sets they were to attempt to reach the top of the mountain in just one day from the South Col with John Hunt supporting them on the South-East Ridge. Two days later, on 25 May, the second assault party, consisting of Ed Hillary and Tenzing, supported by George Lowe, the Sherpa Ang Nima and myself, also left for the South Col.

As I climbed the steep ice of the Lhotse Face with Ed Hillary, Tenzing and George Lowe on the morning of 25 May there was an atmosphere of excitement, a feeling that 'this was it' – at last we were going for the top. As we came to the point where the angle of the slope eventually became less steep, I was brought to a halt by a shout from George. Turning round, I saw that he was jumping up and down with excitement and pointing towards the top of Everest. It was one of the most thrilling moments of the whole expedition for high on the white snow there were two tiny dots and they were moving upwards. They were Tom and Charles going over the South Summit, the two highest men ever on a mountain, and it really seemed as though they were on their way to the top. And so it was with great anticipation that we arrived at the South Col and met John Hunt who, with his Sherpa Da Namgyal, had been up to 27,500 feet in support of Charles and Tom and had left stores which were part of the gear for Hillary and Tenzing's summit attempt.

Charles and Tom had climbed the South Peak of Everest, higher than man had ever been before but, alas, they could go no further. We could not see them during their descent but late in the afternoon they appeared a long way off at the foot of the

South-East Ridge, two small figures creeping back over the ice towards our camp. I photographed them across the wilderness of the South Col, two black shapes on the ice, strangely poignant amidst the emptiness and isolation of that place below the South Summit, which was now concealed in cloud. They came in very, very slowly, the two tiredest men I had ever seen. In their utter weariness they sat down every few yards, and ever so slowly they crept towards us. As I photographed them, I thought it was very strange that they had to stop so often when they were so very near our camp. At least I thought it strange until two days later when I, too, was sitting down in exactly the same way, totally exhausted from the effort required at this altitude.

It is easy to be wise after the event but I have always thought about what might have happened if a high camp has been put up at 28,000 feet for Tom and Charles. Would history have been changed and the first ascent of Everest have been made by Bourdillon and Evans?

The events of the next few days are part of history. But 28 May 1953 must stand out as the most important day of my life when, along with Ang Nima and George Lowe, I climbed the South-East Ridge of Everest ahead of Ed Hillary and Tenzing. Our job was to make the route in preparation for their summit attempt. We stopped to rest at 27,300 feet where I photographed Hillary and Tenzing coming up to join us. They looked terrific, set against the snowy background of Lhotse and Nuptse as they climbed towards me out of the couloir, and the photos I shot then are among the most memorable I took on the expedition. Two hundred feet higher we picked up the stores left on the ridge by John Hunt and Da Namgyal and added them to our load before we continued climbing the South-East Ridge, all of us now carrying 25 to 30 kilos. Here we finally established the highest camp ever placed on a mountain and the following day

Hillary and Tenzing went on to reach the top of Everest.

About half-way down during our return to the South Col, my oxygen supply ran out and exhaustion quickly took over; I could hardly believe it but it became evident that I must discard my oxygen bottle and struggle back without it. George Lowe had enough and as we approached camp it was obvious that he was going better than I was: he seemed to fly to the tent from where he brought out a lightweight cine camera and shot those memorable sequences seen in the Everest film of a very weary Gregory dragging himself extremely slowly across the South Col.

'Was it hard? Was I tired going up?' Now forty years later I am not sure and I don't recall the true hardship of moving upwards in the rarefied air. But what I do remember is the thrill of taking part in a great adventure, the sheer delight of being there and sharing those days with a bunch of very tough men. High on Everest it all seemed certain and I sensed no doubt about the result; I always felt we were going to the top and this would be something which would stay with us for ever.

Spring was always the ideal time for an attempt on Everest, for then the weather is becoming warmer; towards the end of May there is usually a period when conditions are right for a push to the top. It was exactly like this for us. Nowadays Everest is climbed almost throughout the year but improvements in equipment and increased knowledge of the conditions have contributed to this. Back in 1953 we went at the time of year when the weather was most likely to be at its best.

There was great beauty brought by spring to the harsh cold realm of Khumbu. As the snow melted, water sparkled and glistened by the side of the paths and flowers were making their first appearance; there were primulas, irises, gentians and rhododendrons. I remember walking from Khumjung high above the ravine where far below the Imja Khola, no more than a ribbon of white foam flecked with blue light, roared down from the glaciers of the world's highest peaks, and as I climbed the next hill the aroma of crushed pine needles strewn on the path mingled with scent from the blooms of the rhododendrons.

Through the gaps in the trees where new fresh green foliage was breaking out there were visions of snow peaks, and above the yak pastures rose the ice spires of Kang Taiga, Thamserku and Cholatse. Snow pigeons wheeled in a white cloud above my head and the lammergeir vulture soared past, wing tips brushing the trees. On a ridge above the river and within sight of Everest itself, the important Buddhist monastery of Thyangboche guarded the pathway to the mountains, and all around the valleys and hillsides were painted in shades of red and pink by tall trees of flowering rhododendrons. As I wandered along the path past clusters of the stone houses of the Sherpas, I was lost in the beauty of it all and spent many long hours attempting to record on film all that I saw.

I walked along ancient tracks where Sherpas and their families took their yak herds up to spend the summer at the high grazing grounds. Here they would stay where the feed was good, living below some of the world's most magnificent snow and ice peaks. The Sherpas did not have names for the high mountains because they never went to them; there was no reason to go into a forbidding world of snow and ice so these mountains which attracted us were merely the backdrop to the pastures.

The spring weather certainly brought something very special to the Himalaya and I tried to capture the essence of fleeting beauty as the clouds chased the wind across the slopes and danced with shafts of sunlight in front of sensational ice peaks. It often snowed in the afternoon, as indeed it can anywhere in high mountains, and in Khumbu this white miracle created a special kind of magic. As night came the clouds which brought the snowfall dispersed, leaving behind a sky of incredible beauty with millions of stars shining in the velvet black firmament. Such nights were an unforgettable experience. But perhaps it was the early morning which provided the real glory of high Himal when, as the sun rose above an ice ridge, dazzling light shone across the newly fallen snow, as yet unmarked by footprints, and each tiny crystal sparkled like a diamond. Above our camps rose Lhotse, Nuptse, Pumori or Lingtren, all gleaming white, their glittering, glistening walls of ice reaching heavenwards to touch a blue, blue sky.

I had another job apart from the photography – I was the expedition 'postman'. This fitted in well with my need to send film with the 'runners' who carried our mail to Kathmandu. And what athletes these men were! James Morris, the *Times* correspondent, paid them special bonus rates if they could reach Kathmandu particularly quickly with his dispatches, and some record runs were made. My postal duties required me to sort out the incoming mail and to collect letters from members of the team which they wanted to send home. The officer at the Indian post office in Kathmandu (the only one there in those days) was a bit of a rogue and I suspected he showed our cards and telegrams to the press. However, I rather liked him and was delighted when we decided to give him an attractive square of carpet to use as a cushion on his hard chair in recognition of his service to us. Two years later when I returned to Kathmandu I found he had framed it and it now hung on the post office wall with a suitable inscription to say it had been given by the British Everest Expedition.

In camps on the mountain conversation was inevitably about climbing and when we shared a tent with the New Zealanders we rock men from Britain would be the first to

Thyangboche Gompa with Everest in the background.

talk endlessly about hard routes in Lakeland or on Welsh crags. Eventually the Kiwis would get a word in and tell spellbinding tales of the New Zealand Alps. Sometimes we might talk of equipment and the type of gear they used in their country, and I was always intrigued by their ice axes – compared with ours, and mine in particular, they were extremely long. But when it came to using them on a long ice slope both George and Ed wielded them in a masterly way, using two hands as they hacked out enormous steps.

For them there was no way of using an axe in the Alpine style, as I had learned while guiding parties in France and Switzerland, when with one hand a step could be sliced out of snow ice as you continually moved upwards – it was a different world! A young climbing friend of mine recently said, 'I have been looking at a picture of Hillary and Lowe at the South Col – they seemed to be carrying poles!'

During the hours spent in lonely mountain campsites it was possible to have some understanding of how each one of us felt about mountains. Some considered a mountain just as something to climb, a challenge, a setting for high adventure with its attendant danger. It was not a goddess of the snows nor was it anything which would affect them personally. Others felt the summit of Everest was an entity, a 'something' which could influence their lives. Wilf Noyce and John Hunt, I am sure, thought like this. I firmly believed all mountains had the power to teach sharp lessons and perhaps even to kill if approached without due respect and reverence. Not for nothing did we, like the Sherpas, recite the mantra of the Boddhisatva of Compassion, Avalokitesvara: 'Om mani padme hum.' When we were back in Kathmandu after the climb the Nepalese would continually ask Tenzing, 'At the summit, did you meet Lord Shiva? Did you see Lord Buddha?' Certainly I could not have come back from the top and said, 'Well, we knocked the bastard off,' as Ed did.

On several occasions I found myself wondering exactly what the expedition was all about and what we were doing there. The attempt to climb Everest had been going on for a long time, ever since 1921, and there had been so many failures. All those earlier expeditions thought they, too, would reach the top, and they didn't. Why should we expect to do it after all these failures? Yet I felt we would be successful, and the higher we went on the mountain the more I sensed that this very determined team would get there. There was something special about this group of climbers, all of whom on other peaks were leaders in their own right. They were determined to do everything possible to make certain somebody, it did not matter who, reached the summit. For all this, the greatest possible credit goes to John Hunt for the way he led and inspired us. A great bond of friendship developed between us all and this has continued unabated ever since. Sadly, not all expeditions have been so fortunate. Perhaps we were the last of the old-time mountaineers when we truly climbed as a team and commercialism had not yet been introduced to the mountains.

*   *   *

It was in the Western Cwm that my outlook on photography started to change. I began to see a beauty in the immediate mountain landscape, the splendour of a pure white world tinged by grey rock, sometimes blurred by a whirling blizzard and the perspective flattened by falling snowflakes. When the sun was shining the glare was fierce and the snow and ice shimmered so that nothing could be seen except, perhaps, the dark edge of a crevasse or the outline of climbers moving in front of me, only half visible in the blazing light. Here I had a first hint that I was moving away from the pictorial approach to landscape photography, especially in monochrome, and I began to see this story as one of dark against light, of black shapes of men moving slowly, very slowly, towards the summit.

Photographically, what I was seeing had to do with things in space and the space made by things, the isolation of climbers against a pure white wilderness. For me it became all-important to try to see this as a two-dimensional image, ignoring perspective and three-dimensional form, for out in front of the camera everything was white, a flat canvas against which outlines in black became abstract shapes. It became important for me to shoot for high contrast in terms of exposure, for in this medium white snow must be white.

Today there is much talk about photography as an art form and there is a strong movement of Contemporary Photography which is much talked about in certain circles. Some of its main exponents are producing work of great originality, but many others try to jump on the bandwagon with the masters and end up producing photos which are utterly dreary. Pictures from Everest were 'contemporary' in their day – but things move on. A picture reflects the thoughts of the photographer and his perceptive eye. Let me quote something which I wrote for a photographic journal twenty-eight years ago:

It seems to me 'The Perceptive Eye' sums up what photography is all about, its way of working and seeing. The end product becomes a picture with vision. Far away and beyond the accepted and so often corny concepts of pictorialism lies a world of fantasy and emotional depth which a photographer can take if he sees it, and through his camera make it say something of his own thoughts and philosophy.

I think it means seeing through the outward appearance of the ordinary and the humdrum scene and turning it inside out so as to present the other side of the looking-glass to show a realm of fantasy and its dream quality, and to present it so that it becomes the true and only reality. It is a moment in time, a thought blown by the wind, a shadow on a wall or colour at high noon. Beauty is in the eye of the beholder they say, but 'The Perceptive Eye' is born in a realization of the abstract quality of things.

Somewhere in the commentary I gave in the BBC film, *The Other Side of the Mountain*, made for the twenty-fifth anniversary of our climb, I said, 'The twenty-ninth of May 1953 was the first day of the rest of our lives,' and so it was to be.

I went to Everest a keen amateur photographer but I came back a 'pro' and since then I have been able to travel to most countries of the earth and to live the life of a professional photographer. For twenty years I worked freelance for Kodak, giving lectures and big photo presentations with my Kodachrome pictures taken in remote corners of the earth; with my wife, Sue, I regularly presented two screen audio-visual shows. Photography became a way of life and I cannot imagine going anywhere without making images of the lands I visit.

There is always the unexpected just around the corner and so my search goes on to find that elusive quality which can have a much deeper meaning and add some statement to the art of photography. Over the years I feel I have almost found this in my pictures of people where my camera has portrayed them laughing or crying, and occasionally my lens has looked into their eyes to show a little of what was in their hearts. However, the high peaks still call and by the time this book is published Sue and I hope to be away once more in a remote corner of the Himalaya, not in Khumbu but in a secret corner of Nepal that I used to know before 'my Everest'.

Alfred Gregory
Peak District, 1992

The Sherpani wife of one of our porters, with her new baby.

An unnamed peak at the head of the Tolam Bau
Glacier.

MY FIRST HIMALAYAN EXPEDITION IN 1952

I first saw the great peaks of Khumbu from above the Tolam Bau Glacier to the west of Everest. This spectacular unexplored country made a very great impression on me and drew me back in 1955.

The Sherpa village of Thame, where Tenzing was
born, is situated below the Langmoche La.

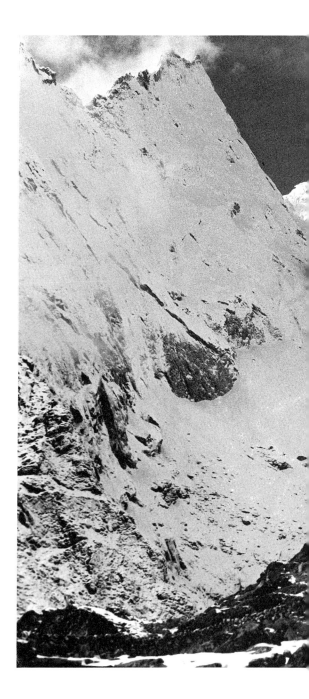

Cho Oyu and Gyachung Kang, seen from the
Tolam Bau Glacier.

My first view of Everest, Lhotse and Makalu seen from the Tolam Bau.

Durbar Square, Kathmandu. This great temple
complex where more than fifty monuments and
temples are found, is situated just outside the
gateway to the former Royal Palace in the centre
of the city. Today it is thronged with both
Nepalese and tourists but in the 1950s it was a
quiet, peaceful place where the devout
worshipped daily.

KATHMANDU

Nepal had been closed to the outside world for 104 years under the rule of the Rana Prime Ministers, and when I first arrived in Kathmandu after the 1952 expedition with Eric Shipton, I was in a capital city virtually unchanged for centuries. In Durbar Square, just outside the Royal Palace, the images of King Pratap Malla with his consorts, high on their plinth, watched over a quiet and peaceful city centre where traffic was non-existent. Kathmandu was little more than a big village where Western influences had not yet made their mark. Everyone wore traditional clothing; T-shirts and jeans were then unknown.

One of the many vegetable stalls where city
dwellers could purchase fresh produce which
farmers carried into town before dawn and
displayed on the tiered base of a temple. A
waistcoat or jacket over a long shirt worn outside
the trousers was the normal dress for the men and
very few people wore shoes.

Two girls and two puppies pause in their play in a side street near Durbar Square. Toys were not known and a younger child spent the day in the care of an older brother or sister.

A young girl rests on the steps of a Hindu temple. At her side is a *doka*, or basket, which is carried on the back by means of a headband. When the basket has become worn it is not thrown away but inverted and used as a chicken coop.

A street which knew neither traffic nor tourists.
A man carries a bundle of wood for cooking fuel
past houses and shops. Simple clay bricks were
used as building material and doorways and
windows were outlined in wood, often intricately
carved. The roofs of the houses reflect the pagoda
architecture of the temples.

The three-tiered roof of Kasi Biswanath Temple, dedicated to Bhairab, rises above Taumadi Tole in the nearby town of Bhaktapur, known as the City of Devotees. The small image of Bhairav housed within the structure is paraded through the streets during the annual Bisket festival. Bhaktapur, also known as Bhadgaon, lies on the ancient trade route from Kathmandu to Tibet and it was from here that we left to walk to Khumbu.

The temple to the extreme left of the picture is now a café for the tourists.

All our expedition stores were assembled on the
Nepalese Army's parade ground on the outskirts
of Bhaktapur and here the porters gathered before
setting off with their loads on the march to
Thyangboche in Khumbu.

THE APPROACH MARCH

In 1953 we walked from Kathmandu to Everest – and back. The mountain is about 175 miles from the valley of Kathmandu and we took seventeen days to reach Thyangboche, where we made our first base camp. The term 'trekking' for a walk in Himalaya was never used in 1953 but today the walk to Everest Base Camp is one of the most popular treks in Nepal. For us it was a glorious walking holiday as we wandered across foothill ridges through some of the most beautiful country in the world.

Local porters were employed, and each carried 30 kilos together with his own blanket, cooking pot and food. Our stages were governed by the distance the porters covered each day, which was about 12 miles. Often travelling barefoot across rough tracks, the only trade routes in a land without roads, they were part of a tradition which still continues: there are still no roads to Khumbu and all stores must be carried on the backs of men.

Each day we started early and walked for a couple of hours before our breakfast halt. The weather was hot and George Band wore a smart panama hat. We climbed many ridges separated by deep valleys and on the upper slopes the rhododendrons were blooming. As we went higher and reached the Sherpa country of Khumbu we passed many *mani* walls where the Buddhist prayer '*Om mani padme hum*' was carved into the rock. In keeping with tradition we always passed by with these walls to our right-hand side. Sherpa children would come to watch us as we walked through their isolated villages.

Porters moving away from one of our campsites in the foothills. After an early cup of tea and a bar of chocolate we would pack our gear and leave, not having breakfast until we stopped some time later. To take advantage of the beautiful light at this time of the day I always tried to go with the porters to look for pictures as they walked out through the forest where the low light filtering through the trees cast long shadows and the background hills were bathed in soft mist.

Bridges like this are still found throughout the foothills, although more substantial structures have replaced the old ones on the busier routes used by today's trekkers. To build each bridge all the materials have to be carried through the mountains on the backs of men and although many of the bridges fall into a poor state of repair and so make for exciting crossings they are essential for the hill people when the rivers are in spate during the monsoon season.

(Left) Two of our porters cooking breakfast.

(Below left) Our mess tent. Wilf Noyce is drinking from his personalized mug; behind him is Tom Stobart. George Lowe sits in the middle and on the right Tom Bourdillon relaxes in front of George Band.

(Right) Sherpa boy pulling on Tibetan-style boots.

(Below right) Sherpa children from Khumbu. Today, trainers have replaced the Tibetan boots, and jeans and T-shirts are everywhere.

A Sherpani weaving with yak wool.

(Left above) Mist in the rhododendron forest.

(Left below) '*Om mani padme hum.*'

The route to Everest ran through the high valleys of Khumbu and as we approached Thyangboche we saw the black triangle of Everest above the long Nuptse ridge. On the right is Lhotse, and Taweche rises above the Sherpa village of Phortse laid out on a flat area near the centre of the picture. Sherpas live here throughout the year and take their yaks to summer grazing in the higher valleys.

Campsite at Thyangboche.

ACCLIMATIZATION AND EXPLORATION

We camped for about a month in a beautiful grassy area very close to the Thyangboche *gompa*, or monastery, at 12,687 feet. The *gompa*, a most attractive place built in Tibetan style, was recently destroyed by a fire started by an electric heater; the arrival of electricity has been a mixed blessing. I wonder what became of the empty oxygen cylinder used as a gong for the call to prayer; it originally came from an early Everest expedition from the north side of the mountain and was brought across from the monastery at Rongbuk.

Birches, firs and rhododendron forest covered the slopes around our camp and the view of the mountains was breathtaking. Ama Dablam, 22,493 feet, Lhotse, 27,890 feet, Nuptse, 25,850 feet, and Everest, 29,029 feet, were before us whilst almost above rose the fantastic ice ridges of Kang Taiga, 22,241 feet, and Thamserku, 21,680 feet. Everywhere I looked there were majestic ice-fluted peaks where morning sunlight caressed the high snows and swirling afternoon clouds played around their tops making them appear higher than ever. On some mornings we woke to find a light mantle of snow covering the tents but it soon melted in the warm sunshine.

We used our time here for acclimatization and exploration and I went up twice to climb above Chhukhung in the Imja Khola Valley. On one occasion, Charles Evans, Charles Wylie, Tenzing and I made the first ascent of an attractive mountain, just over 20,000 feet. It was called Island Peak and today it is climbed by more people than any other mountain in Nepal.

Low cloud and fresh snow painted with early
morning light.

A blue-black sky and seemingly bottomless foreground frame a high mountain wall of rock and ice. Silver clouds continually flow over the ridges creating abstract patterns of their own. Mountains are so often wrapped in cloud and I feel they should be photographed this way: when the cloud cover starts to break up it often produces a mystic quality so special in this high country.

In 1953 the peaks of Khumbu were a vast pristine wilderness area and our presence amongst them was virtually insignificant. For the Nepalese, and particularly the Sherpas who grazed their yaks in the high windswept valleys, these areas were truly the Abode of the Gods. My camera could merely record the light and shadow on the clouds which swirled across the peaks and ridges to convey an aura of spirituality which I felt was certainly present.

The permanent snow and ice of Ama Dablam dominated our view during this acclimatization period and so it continually presented a photographic challenge. After a fresh snowfall the mountain appeared remote and serene high above the stippled foreground where running water formed ink-black stripes across the pastures.

George Band and John Hunt testing one of the radio sets.

(Left) Kang Taiga. When the clouds rolled out of the valleys as evening approached, the jagged edge of Kang Taiga appeared as if suspended in space and time, seemingly higher than ever.

Island Peak. This fine peak stands isolated in the Imja Valley and so was a natural choice for us to climb during the acclimatization period.

Charles Wylie looking at the ice-fluted peaks above the Imja Glacier during our first ascent of Island Peak.

From our camp on the ridge of Island Peak we
looked west to snow-clad peaks stretching as far
as the eye could see.

As we left Thyangboche the summit of Everest
dropped behind the wall of Nuptse.

WALK TO BASE CAMP

After our acclimatization period we set off for Everest. We walked through the villages of Pangboche and Pheriche and then climbed up past Duglha to the Khumbu Glacier. Today this glacier is virtually unrecognizable as it has greatly receded and most of the huge ice pinnacles, or seracs, have disappeared. Our 'Lake Camp' is known locally as Gorak Shep, and Base Camp, situated at about 17,900 feet to the right of the Khumbu Icefall, was much lower down the glacier than the place known today as Everest Base Camp. Our tents, pitched on stones surrounded by huge seracs, were often completely hidden by the ice and so it became quite difficult to locate the camp.

From Thyangboche we only used Sherpa porters. This strong, sturdy race of people, originally from Tibet, who now inhabit Khumbu, were used to living at this altitude and were adapted to the low temperatures. Both men and women carried loads and entire families came with us. They always appeared immensely happy and cheerful, and it seemed that the harder the conditions became the more they would laugh. We had a period of unsettled weather when snow fell each afternoon making the porters' work considerably more arduous.

From Base Camp we looked across a cirque of magnificent mountains: Pumori 23,442 feet, Lingtren 21,971 feet, Khumbutse 21,784 feet, Changtse 24,770 feet and the deceptively easy-looking col on the Tibetan border, the Lho La, 19,705 feet, across which avalanches fell from the cliffs above.

Sherpa porters took over the load-carrying from the lowland porters when we reached the higher altitudes, and here at Pheriche a group gathers before moving off at the start of the day. In the background we had our last glimpse of Kang Taiga and Thamserku before the great mountains at the head of Khumbu surrounded us.

A spring snowfall in the yak pastures near
Pheriche. These animals have been brought up
from the lower villages to spend the summer
months where there is good grazing. They are
indispensable beasts to the Sherpa communities,
providing them with milk and wool, and they are
also extremely capable at carrying loads. Even in
deep snow yaks move well and are often used to
break a trail. Yaks must live at altitude as they
cannot survive the warmer temperatures in the
lower regions.

A baby yak with its mother in a snowstorm.

The porters' kitchen at Lake Camp, now known
as Gorak Shep. In between the stones of the
moraine the hardy Sherpas set up their cooking
fires and when darkness falls they snuggle down
nearby to spend the night.

Before leaving Lake Camp for Base Camp Charles
Evans issued snow goggles to the Sherpa porters.
We were worried about the possibility of
snowblindness and so we hastily made some extra
goggles out of cardboard. Many of the men,
however, preferred their own method of pulling
their long plait of hair across their eyes and
peering through it.

Sherpa porters approaching Base Camp at the end
of the carry from Thyangboche. While we were
on the mountain these Sherpas returned to their
homes in the Namche district of Khumbu and
when it was time for us to leave they came back
up to Base Camp to carry our equipment away.

Flying over Base Camp is the Union Jack which
we pitched on the Khumbu Glacier close to the
foot of the Icefall. Above Tenzing's tent flutters his
personal mascot. There was always a welcome for
weary climbers returning here from the higher
camps and Thondup, our cook, would spoil us
with fresh food and good mutton. There was the
added bonus of the possibility that a runner may
have arrived from Kathmandu with mail from
home.

Boxes of stores lie round a tent at Base Camp
which is overshadowed by the ice of the Khumbu
Glacier and the peak of Lingtren.

George Band, Ed Hillary, Charles Evans, Mike Ward and Tom Stobart in the 'Himalayan Position' in the mess tent. On all expeditions much time is spent lying in a tent. As the great explorer and climber, Bill Tilman, so wisely said, 'The occupational disease of Himalayan climbers is bed sores!'

Charles Evans and George Lowe at Base Camp.

John Hunt putting on crampons.

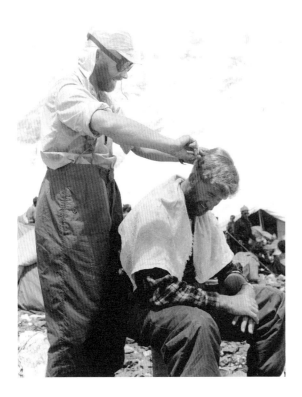

Figures leaving Base Camp for the Icefall are
dwarfed by a great cathedral-like ice pinnacle on
the glacier. Changtse, across the border in Tibet,
and the uncrossed col of the Lho La are in the
background. Today these great seracs have gone
with the retreating of the glacier.

Sunlight shining on ice pinnacles created a magic of its own and made this high remote corner of the earth one of the most beautiful places in the world. The ice of the Lho La and the West Ridge of Everest, still mainly in shadow, present an awe-inspiring backdrop.

THE KHUMBU ICEFALL

To carry about three tons of stores up the Icefall and into the Western Cwm we employed thirty-four Sherpa porters, all properly clothed and equipped for high altitude. A member of the team escorted each group through the frightening labyrinth of moving blocks of ice, and we fixed ropes and ladders to ease the passage up the steepest pitches.

This formidable place, made even more terrifying by the continual movement of the glacier, was both beautiful and awe-inspiring in its chaos. In the midst of this tortuous jumble, blue-green walls of ice dropped away into the bottomless abyss of a crevasse whilst above the precipitous seracs towering over me I could see a sky of intense blue.

We pitched Camp 2 half-way up the Icefall but later abandoned it because it was so unsafe. As we returned after the mountain had been climbed, the place where the camp had been was a mass of crevasses and blocks of ice. After negotiating such hazards as 'The Atom Bomb Area', 'The Nutcracker' and 'Mike's Horror', we faced the steepest ice wall of all which brought us into the Western Cwm. Here we placed a rope ladder over this final wall.

(Left) The chaotic mass of moving ice towers menacingly over the porters at the foot of the Icefall.

The great confusion of the Icefall pours down
from the Western Cwm, grinding and moving its
way to the valley below. We made a route
through the middle of this tortuous terrain to
avoid ice avalanches from the mountain walls on
either side.

Two Sherpas in 'Mike's Horror', a fearsome place named after Mike Ward who first led the route through it.

Charles Wylie and a Sherpa descend the Icefall. At this period many of the team spent several days escorting Sherpa porters carrying loads to Camp 3, from where they returned back through the Icefall to Base Camp where another load of stores awaited.

Sherpa porters are carrying tents and boxes of rations to establish our higher camps. They are climbing a steep pitch of ice where we had fixed a rope. The daily work of ferrying stores up the Icefall was often undertaken in adverse conditions as snow fell every afternoon, obliterating the route and making every movement much more arduous. In spite of this we never lost a day.

A Sherpa on the rope ladder, which was a pot-
holing ladder donated by the Yorkshire Ramblers
Club.

The upper part of the Icefall seen from Camp 2. Sleeping here was frightening when the ice shook underneath the tent and great cracks broke the silence as the glacier moved relentlessly down the mountain. The stretch of the Icefall above this camp was a little less steep than below but it was perhaps more dangerous as the blocks of ice were even bigger than those we had already passed.

Tenzing's personal flag flies above Camp 2. Whilst we were establishing Camp 3 we slept half-way up the Icefall but we were not sorry when the Sherpas told us they would prefer to go all the way to Camp 3 rather than spend a night here.

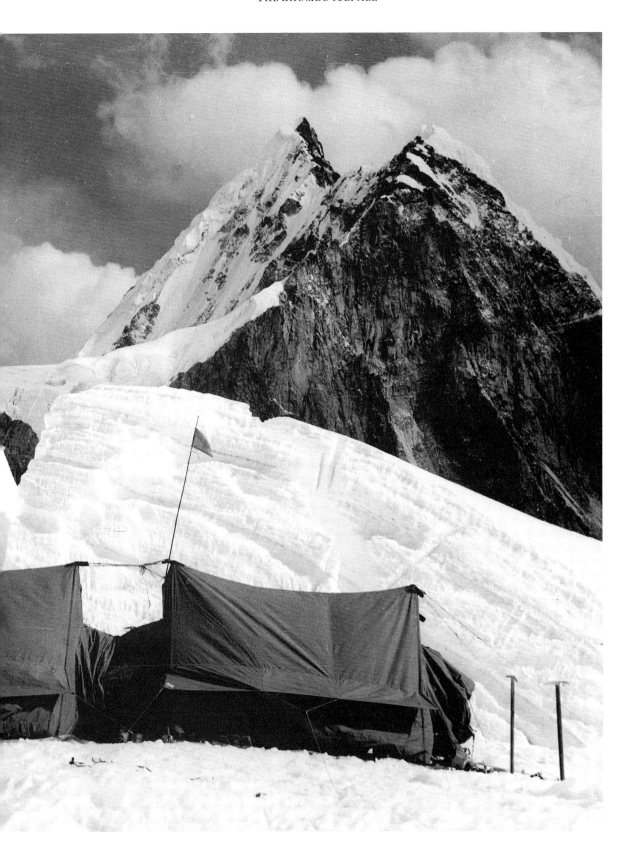

George Lowe stands above an ice wall which John Hunt is climbing. Every step in the Icefall was hazardous and it was weary work negotiating difficulties such as 'The Atom Bomb Area' and 'The Nutcracker'. Perhaps the gods were on our side as we all came through without accident.

Tenzing safeguards a porter during the descent of
the great ice wall at the top of the Icefall as they
begin their descent to Base Camp from Camp 3.
As I photographed them on this precipitous ice
barrier I was very much aware of the intensity of
the blue sky beyond, so deep in colour I knew it
would appear as a dense black when I printed the
negative.

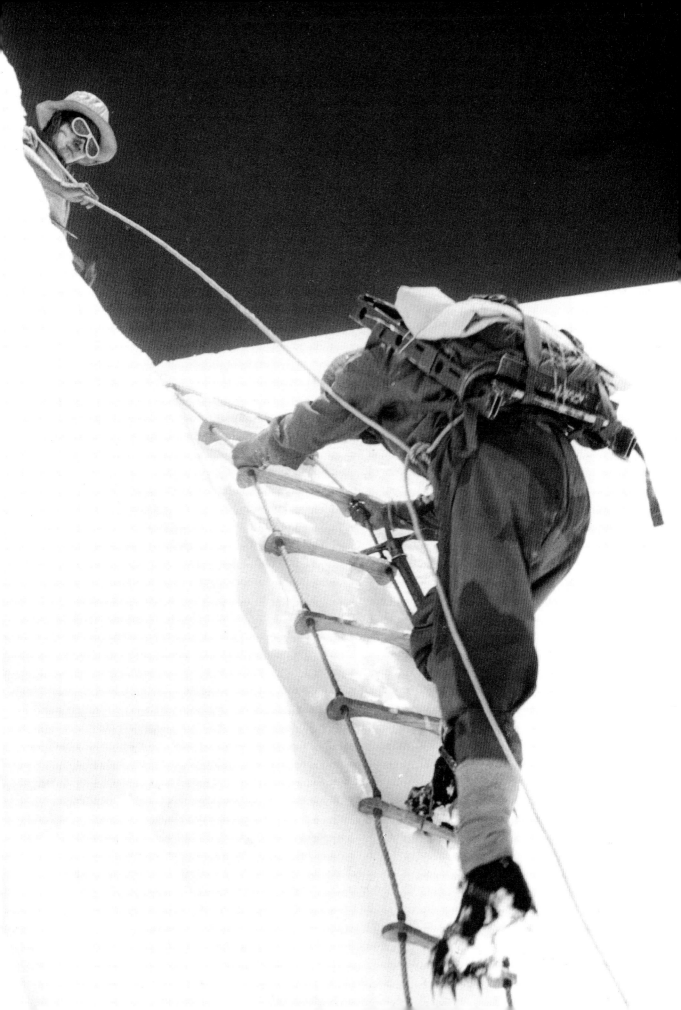

The fierce abstract beauty of the Icefall. Man seemed truly insignificant in these awe-inspiring surroundings where every day the terrain changed completely and menace was ever present.

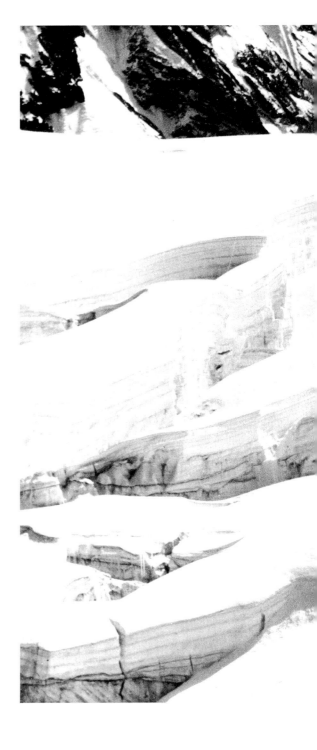

Wilf Noyce, holding marker flags, with our Sherpa
porters at Camp 3.

Camp 3 and the Western Cwm

Camp 3 was pitched at the top of the Icefall at the entrance to the vast wilderness of the Western Cwm. Just above the camp there was the biggest crevasse of all. It was here that the Icefall was beginning to break away from the glacier of the Cwm leaving a massive gap into which fell enormous blocks of ice: this made the crossing very complicated indeed.

For about a week Wilf Noyce, the Sherpas and I ferried stores across this white desert, placing marker flags to indicate our route. When the sun was shining it became incredibly hot, making the going very hard in the softened snow. Returning in the afternoon when the regular snowfall had obliterated our tracks, we were very glad of the flags to guide us safely back to our camp.

The youngest Sherpa, Nawang Gombu, crawls across the alloy ladder spanning the big crevasse. Around his neck is my Kodak Retina 2 camera. Nawang was a student monk at the Rombuk Monastery in Tibet when he heard of our expedition and, as he says, 'I ran away from school to join you.'

The huge crevasse above Camp 3 was bridged by
a light alloy sectional ladder. Wilf Noyce,
crawling across, and his Sherpa team are dwarfed
by the immensity of this crevasse whilst
underneath lies a chaotic jumble of great blocks
of ice and blue-green walls dropping away into
the abyss below.

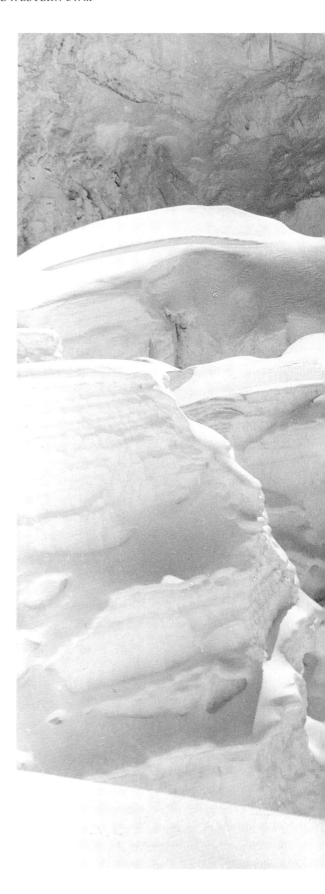

The jagged edge of another crevasse higher in the Western Cwm is negotiated by Wilf Noyce as he leads a group of porters to Camp 4.

The lonely beauty of the Western Cwm.

Wilf Noyce leads a Sherpa along the marked route
through the maze of crevasses in the Western
Cwm. The afternoon snowfalls would obliterate
our footprints and each morning we were faced
with exceedingly hot and tiring work as we beat
another trail through the soft new snow,
following the marker flags around crevasses.

The sheen on the ice of the Lhotse Face glistens
in the hot sun as Wilf Noyce and the Sherpas
move towards Camp 4.

ADVANCE BASE CAMP AND THE LHOTSE FACE

We prepared for the final assault from Camp 4 which was our Advance Base Camp. Lhotse, 27,890 feet, soared above our tents but our eyes turned continually to the granite wall which rose to the South Summit of Everest. Below us the white waves of the glacier flowed down to where the Cwm narrowed before the Icefall fell steeply away. We camped about a mile from the Lhotse Face which presented us with 4,000 feet of difficult ice climbing before we could reach the South Col.

(Left) Tom Stobart with his Bell Howell cine camera.

Advance Base Camp at 21,200 feet.

Tom Bourdillon's high altitude boots. We all had specially made boots in what was then a revolutionary design : thirty-three pairs were produced in Kettering for the team and the high altitude Sherpas. The Himalayan Club in Darjeeling sent diagrams and measurements and special lasts were made for the Sherpas as they had short and very broad feet. The boots were excellent and we used them constantly from Camp 3 onwards.

(Left above) Annallu Sherpa putting on high altitude boots.

(Left below) Pasang Phutar Sherpa putting on crampons.

A Sherpa with an oxygen set.

FIRST AND SECOND ASSAULTS ON THE SUMMIT

These pictures tell my story from 21 May when the attempts on the summit began. The two assault parties set off to climb the steep Lhotse Face to the South Col three days apart. There was one camp before we reached the South Col at 26,218 feet, a most desolate place.

But we were now, hopefully, within reach of the top of Mount Everest and I arrived at the Col buoyed up with excitement as I had seen Tom Bourdillon and Charles Evans going over the top of the South Summit. The first assault had begun.

The action on the mountain, leading up to the eventual success on 29 May, took place from the South Col, along the South-East Ridge and over the South Summit. Beyond the South Summit is the famous Hillary Step which gives access to the final ridge of Everest.

(Left) Sherpa porters, led by Charles Wylie, leaving with the first lift of stores up the Lhotse Face to the South Col.

Tom Bourdillon and Charles Evans, using closed-circuit oxygen sets, leave Advance Base Camp to climb the Lhotse Face to the South Col for the first summit attempt. This experimental oxygen system recycled the air they breathed; the rest of us used the normal pure oxygen in a bottle. We all wished them well and I was already looking forward to following them two days later to the South Col.

It is 25 May and we are off – the second assault
has begun and here Ed Hillary, followed by
Tenzing, leaves Advance Base Camp. I
photographed them as they started up the Lhotse
Face before I followed with a team of Sherpas
carrying more stores to the Col.

Ed Hillary at the camp half-way up the Lhotse Face. Here we spent one night and already we seemed to be at the same height as some of the other great peaks of Khumbu.

As I set off for the South Col I looked up to the
South Summit of Everest rising 5,000 feet above
us and I wondered how Tom Bourdillon and
Charles Evans were going: today they should be
making their summit attempt. The South Summit
is rather foreshortened in this picture, but it
shows the South Col on the right and the black
line of the Geneva Spur running diagonally across
the Lhotse Face.

Sherpas arriving at the South Col from the Lhotse Face. The top of the Icefall can be seen three miles across the Western Cwm, bounded on the left by the ice wall of Nuptse.

Our windswept campsite at the South Col with oxygen bottles in the foreground. The force of the wind was terrific and on 27 May it was too strong for us to leave the Col to go higher. We found it difficult to sleep here without oxygen so we used a low supply of 'sleeping' oxygen. The Col was a very exposed site, perched on the border between Tibet and Nepal, and up here we felt very isolated from the rest of the team down below.

(Right) Da Namgyal Sherpa, exhausted, arrives back at the South Col camp from 27,500 feet where he and John Hunt had gone in support of Tom Bourdillon and Charles Evans. They had also carried stores for Ed Hillary and Tenzing which we picked up and carried higher two days later.

We had been anxiously awaiting the return of
Tom and Charles to the South Col. Had they
reached the top? There was no means of knowing
what had happened until they arrived back. And
then eventually we saw two tiny figures moving
slowly, ever so slowly, leaning into the rising
wind, just two black dots creeping across the
windswept ice towards us.

The exhaustion clearly shows as Tom and Charles
sit within a few strides of the tents. Today, they
had been the two highest men on earth.

(Left) Extremely tired, yet elated at having been so
close to the highest point, Charles Evans and Tom
Bourdillon come towards camp. Although they
had not been to the top of Everest, they had
climbed 3,000 feet in one day to make the first
ascent of the South Summit.

It was 28 May and the wind had dropped at the South Col, although above us on the South Summit there was cloud and snow plume telling of the gale still blowing up there. The stage was now set for the second assault to begin. As I left the camp I saw the stark shape of the South Summit ahead of me and I had no thought other than wanting to climb high on the ridge, along with my companions, to put the last camp for Hillary and Tenzing as far as possible up the mountain to give them the best chance of reaching the top the next day.

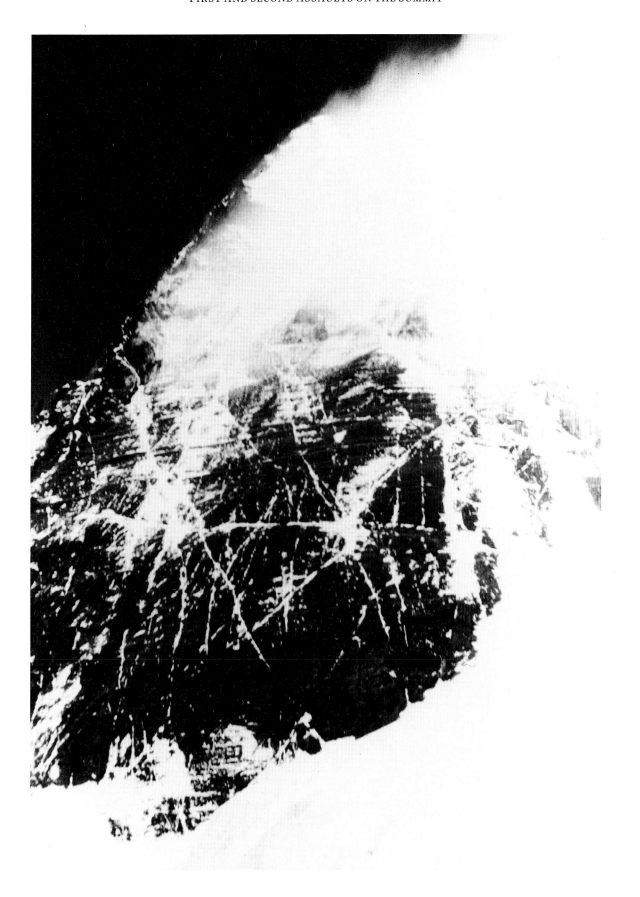

Ed Hillary in front of Tenzing climbs up to where
we waited at 27,300 feet on the South-East Ridge.
We were all carrying loads of over 18 kilos. The
weather was now fine and still and we had
extensive views across Tibet and the mountains of
Nepal.

I photographed Tenzing as he came towards me and, looking at the flags wrapped round his ice axe, I knew there was no doubt about his resolve to get to the top.

George Lowe changes a film at 27,300 feet.

Ang Nima Sherpa turns on his oxygen supply before continuing up the South-East Ridge. Some 200 feet higher we stopped again to take on the stores dumped by John Hunt and Da Namgyal Sherpa and, after some friendly discussion as to who should carry the most awkward loads, we all staggered on up the ridge, each carrying 25–27 kilos.

Ed Hillary and Tenzing on the South-East Ridge on their way to the final camp at 28,000 feet where they spent the night of 28 May before going to the top the next day. It was mid-afternoon when George Lowe, Ang Nima and I turned back to the South Col, leaving Ed and Tenzing to their lonely vigil.

James Morris greets Ed Hillary, back from the top
of Everest, watched by Mike Ward, Tom
Bourdillon, John Hunt and Mike Westmacott.

THE RETURN

There was tremendous excitement amongst us all when Tenzing and Ed Hillary returned from the summit. As well as taking pictures of both Ed and Tenzing I also photographed the groups of men who had been working high on the mountain.

When the entire team was reunited down at Base Camp we gathered round the radio to listen to the Coronation. Imagine our amazement and surprise when we heard that our success on Everest had been announced to the world on Coronation Day.

The two assault parties back together at Advance
Base Camp. Hillary and Tenzing, still roped
together, are flanked by Charles Evans on the left
and Tom Bourdillon. On the extreme right is
George Band.

(Right) Back from the summit – Tenzing and Ed
Hillary pose for an 'official' portrait.

The assault support teams of John Hunt, Da
Namgyal Sherpa, myself, Ang Nima Sherpa and
George Lowe.

The team which made the first carry of stores to
the South Col. Standing, left to right: Nawang
Gombu, Ang Temba, Charles Wylie, Pasang
Phutar, Pasang Dawa, Ang Dorje. In front:
Topke, Pemba, Ang Namgyal, Dawa Tondup.

As we all rejoiced in the knowledge that the mountain had been climbed, I tried to capture something of the relief and relaxation in Ed Hillary as he gratefully drank a hot cup of tea (from Tom Stobart's mug) on his return to Advance Base Camp.

A small section of the crowd from Kathmandu
which came to meet us as we entered the
Kathmandu Valley. In the centre with his back to
me is the British Ambassador, Christopher
Summerhayes, and on his right is a garlanded
John Hunt. Ed Hillary is behind John, and George
Band's panama hat is distinctive. Next to him is
Wilf Noyce. Tenzing is in front of the left-hand flag
with his sunglasses on his hat.

Ed Hillary's face reflects the effort of the previous
weeks as he rests close to Kathmandu.

SHERPAS

Ever since the expedition I have remained friends with many of the Sherpas, meeting them in their homes with their wives and families at regular intervals over the years and sometimes showing something of the Peak District to them when they come to stay with me. Both Tenzing and Nawang, once farmers of yaks, showed enormous fascination and interest in the cows of Britain.

(Top left) Da Namgyal. Together with John Hunt
he carried loads to 27,500 feet.

(Top right) Ang Nima. He was the highest Sherpa
on the mountain apart from Tenzing, when he,
George Lowe and I carried loads up to 27,900
feet.

(Above) Dawa Tenzing. He carried a load to the
South Col. I first met Dawa in 1952 and he was
my Sirdar in 1958; we remained close friends.

(Above right) Annallu. I first met him in 1952
and he became one of my closest friends,
accompanying me on other expeditions. He
carried loads twice to the South Col in 1953.

(Right) Nawang Gombu. Tenzing's nephew and
our youngest Sherpa at about sixteen years of age.
In 1953 he went to the South Col and later
became the first man to climb Everest twice. He
took over from Tenzing at the Himalayan
Institute.

Tenzing Norgay. He became Director of Training
at the Himalayan Institute in Darjeeling.

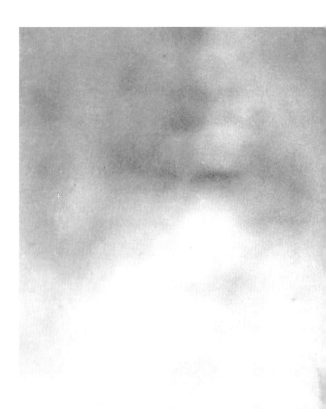

Everest was once the loneliest mountain on earth . . .

. . . until we broke the silence.

As we returned to Kathmandu I saw the great
stupa of Swayambunath, with the all-seeing eyes
of the Buddha gazing out across the valley as they
have for centuries. Swayambu, whose very name
means 'self-existent', is dedicated to the supreme
Adi-Buddha, the primordial Buddha born of the
flame. We had just climbed the highest mountain
in the world, an event of great importance to us
at the time but in reality no more than one small
episode in the whole existence of the universe.

Today, many walk as we did where the gods
once dwelt alone.